With love to our little angel, Zach
~ Mimi

THE WISE ANIMAL HANDBOOK

Kate B. Jerome

ARCADIA KIDS

Attempt new **skills** from **time** to **time.**

Just **try** to think them **through.**

And if you find you're left behind...

...then change your point of view.

Try
not
to
think
of just
yourself.

Invent new ways to **share.**

Stay close to friends whom you can trust.

But
always
be
aware.

Avoid
the
tattle
in the
tale.

Insist that **truth** is **best.**

Embrace with pride the strengths you have.

Demand
to be
impressed.

Enjoy
the
peace
that
nature
brings.

Ignore what's just for **show.**

Join **forces** when the road gets **rough.**

Admit when you don't know.

Remember **family** is the **best.**

Despite the **ups** and **downs.**

Don't **hide** from things that you must **face.**

Make
joyful
laughing
sounds.

Eat **healthy** food to **grow** up **strong.**

Be **patient** with your **friends.**

Try not to take a stubborn stand.

Be **quick** to make amends.

εxcuse yourself when manners slip.

Be helpful every day.

Keep trying even when it's hard.

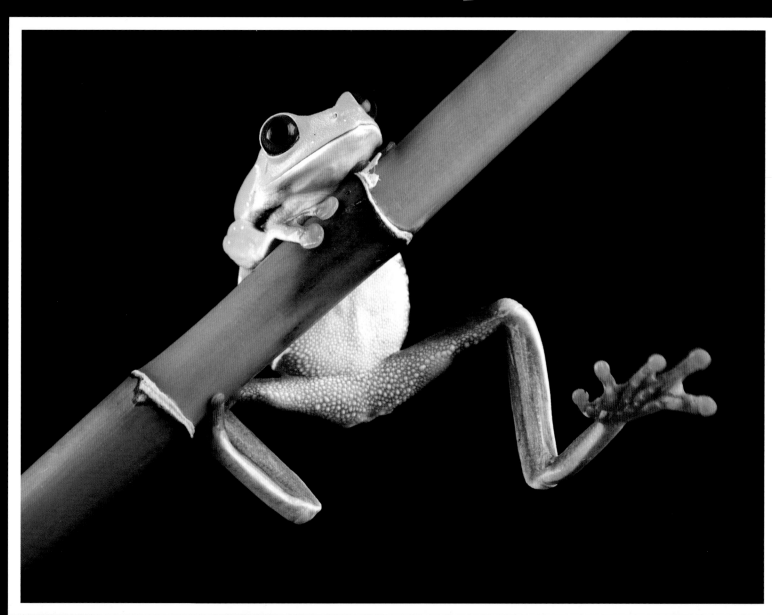

But don't forget to play!

And
sing

...and **dance** each **day!**

Written by Kate B. Jerome
Design and Production: Lumina Datamatics, Inc.
Coloring Illustrations: Tom Pounders
Research: Eric Nyquist

Cover Images: See back cover

Interior Images: 002 Anetapics/Shutterstock.com; 003 George Green/Shutterstock.com; 004 Sergey Uryadnikov/Shutterstock.com; 005 Gnomeandi/Shutterstock.com; 006 Bruce MacQueen/Shutterstock.com; 007 Henk Bentlage/Shutterstock.com; 008 M.M./Shutterstock.com; 009 Mikael Damkier/Shutterstock.com; 010 Brendan van Son/Shutterstock.com; 011 Michael Pettigrew/Shutterstock.com; 012 StevenRussellSmithPhotos/Shutterstock.com; 013 Pakhnyushchy/Shutterstock.com; 014 Patjo/Shutterstock.com; 015 Quinn Martin/Shutterstock.com; 016 Lincoln Rogers/Shutterstock.com; 017 Dirk Ercken/Shutterstock.com; 018 Karel Gallas/Shutterstock.com; 019 Orangecrush/Shutterstock.com; 020 Guenter-foto/Shutterstock.com; 021 Janecat/Shutterstock.com; 022 Shironina/Shutterstock.com; 023 Annette Shaff/Shutterstock.com; 024 Vitaly Titov/Shutterstock.com; 025 Rohappy/Shutterstock.com; 026 MattiaATH/Shutterstock.com; 027 Otsphoto/Shutterstock.com; 028 FikMik/Shutterstock.com; 029 Four Oaks/Shutterstock.com; 030 Ekaterina Kolomeets/Shutterstock.com; 031 Hugh Lansdown/Shutterstock.com.

Published by Arcadia Kids, a division of Arcadia Publishing and
The History Press, Charleston, SC

For all general information contact Arcadia Publishing at:
Telephone: 843-853-2070
Email: sales@arcadiapublishing.com

For Customer Service and Orders:
Toll Free: 1-888-313-2665
Visit us on the Internet at www.arcadiapublishing.com

Library of Congress Cataloging-in-Publication data is on file with the publisher.

Printed in China

Oklahoma State **Butterfly**

Black Swallowtail

Read Together

The black swallowtail was named the state butterfly in 1996. The butterfly can be commonly found in Oklahoma from May to October.

Oklahoma State Animal

American Buffalo

Read Together

The buffalo was named the state animal in 1972. This great animal is seen as symbol for people to protect and preserve the natural environment.

Oklahoma State Game Bird

Wild Turkey

Read Together

The wild turkey was named the state game bird in 1990. Wild turkeys can be found throughout the state—usually nesting under bushes and logs.

© Kate B. Jerome 2017

Oklahoma State **Game Animal**

White-Tailed Deer

Read Together

The white-tailed deer was named "the most beautiful and prized symbol of Oklahoma wildlife" when it became the state game animal in 1990.